J BIO IGLESIAS
Talmadge, Morgan.
Enrique Iglesias /

CELEBRITY BIOS

Enrique Iglesias

Morgan Talmadge

HIGH
interest
books

Children's Press
A Division of Grolier Publishing
New York / London / Hong Kong / Sydney
Danbury, Connecticut

Contributing Editor: Jennifer Ceaser
Book Design: Nelson Sa

Photo Credits: Cover © Mitch Gerber/Corbis; p. 4 © Walter Weissman/Globe Photos Inc.; pp. 6, 8 © Bettmann/Corbis; p. 11 © ClassMates.com Yearbook Archives; pp. 13, 14 © Fitzroy Barrett/Globe Photos Inc.; p. 18 © Sonia Moskowitz/Globe Photos Inc.; p. 21 © Corbis; p. 23 © Globe Photos Inc.; pp. 25, 26 © Reuters NewMedia Inc./Corbis; p. 29 © AFP/Corbis; p. 30 © Reuters NewMedia Inc./Corbis; p. 33 © Lisa Rose/Globe Photos Inc.; p. 35 © Pacha/Corbis; p. 39 © AFP/Corbis.

Library of Congress Cataloging-in-Publication Data

Talmadge, Morgan.
  Enrique Iglesias / by Morgan Talmadge.
  p. cm. (Celebrity bios)
  ISBN 0-516-23417-X (lib. bdg.) – ISBN 0-516-23579-6 (pbk.)
  1. Iglesias, Enrique, vocalist—Juvenile literature. 2. Singers—United States—Biography—Juvenile literature. [1. Iglesias, Enrique, vocalist. 2. Singers. 3.
Hispanic Americans—Biography.] I. Title. II. Series.

ML3930.I39 T35 2000
782.42164'092—dc21
[B]
                                                        00-031670

CONTENTS

CHAPTER ONE

Music In His Blood

"When Enrique was little, if a friend intro-
duced him as Julio Iglesias's son, he would
walk away. He never used [his famous last
name], either in school, or with girls, or
in a restaurant."
> —Fernan Martinez, Enrique's manager,
> in *Teen People*

Enrique Iglesias is one of music's biggest and brightest young stars. His catchy brand of Latin pop has thrilled fans all over the world. He has sold more Spanish-language albums over the past four years than has any other artist. His first English single, "Bailamos,"

Enrique Iglesias is one of Latin pop's biggest stars.

topped the U.S. pop music chart. He's picked up several awards for his music, including a Grammy and an American Music Award. He's recorded a successful duet with Whitney Houston called "Could I Have This Kiss Forever." As of April 2000, Enrique has sold more than seventeen million records.

Though he is the son of world-famous singer Julio Iglesias, Enrique never used his father's name to succeed. Enrique always insisted on making music his way, with his own unique sound and style.

FROM MADRID TO MIAMI

Enrique Iglesias was born in Madrid, Spain, on May 8, 1975. His mother is Isabel Preysler, a Filipino model. His father is Julio Iglesias, one of the most successful Latin singers of all time. Enrique's parents divorced when he was just three years old. His father moved to Miami, Florida, after the divorce. Enrique continued living in Madrid with his mother, his older brother, Julio Jr., and his sister, Chabeli.

When Enrique was seven years old, his grandfather was kidnapped in Madrid. His grandfather was rescued, but the kidnapping made Enrique's parents very nervous. They did not want their children to live in a dangerous place. So Enrique and his siblings moved to Miami to live with their father. Enrique's mother, Isabel, stayed in Spain. Isabel told *People*, "It broke my heart to send [my children] away but we had to for security reasons." Enrique returned to Spain four times

The Iglesias family holds a press conference after learning about the kidnapping of Enrique's grandfather.

a year to spend time with his mother. However, the separation was very difficult for a young boy. Enrique recalled in *InStyle* that "leaving [my mother] was one of the hardest parts of my life."

In Miami, Enrique and his siblings went from being surrounded by bodyguards to being regular kids. Enrique told *Teen People*, "I had a normal life . . . [my father] never spoiled us. He raised us well." Yet, their father often was away on concert tours. So Enrique and his siblings were raised by their nanny, Elvira Olivares. She was a mother figure for the three Iglesias children when they were growing up. Olivares has always been a positive influence in the children's lives, and she and Enrique are still very close. "She took care of us when we were little," Enrique told *Teen People* of Olivares. "[Now] she's my friend." Their friendship would later be crucial to Enrique's success.

This photo shows Enrique with his mom and dad before his first communion.

GROWING UP AMERICAN

In Miami, young Enrique was raised just as any other American kid. He attended an American school. He ate American food. He listened to American music, including Tom Petty, Bruce Springsteen, Billy Joel, and Lionel Richie.

Enrique found comfort in music. He was a shy and lonely boy who spent many hours

listening to his favorite songs. Not only did Enrique listen to music, he also wrote songs and recorded them on a tape recorder. He told the *Buffalo News* that writing music was an outlet for his feelings. "It was the only way I had to express myself. I had nobody to talk to. I'd pick up a piece of paper and write some lyrics."

A YOUNG ARTIST

Throughout his teenage years, Enrique wrote his songs in secret. The first song he wrote was in English. He wrote it when he was thirteen years old. Enrique wrote songs in both Spanish and English, but his plan was to record all of the songs in English.

Finally, when Enrique was seventeen years old, he found the courage to start sharing his songs with other people. He decided to record a demo tape of his music to present to record labels. However, Enrique did not have enough money to pay for the recording and he did not

want his parents to know about his plan to be a musician. He was afraid that they would try to talk him out of it. Instead, Enrique confided in his nanny, Elvira Olivares, who lent him $5,000 to make his first demo tape in 1994.

At that time, Enrique was majoring in business at the University of Miami. He dropped out of college to concentrate on his music. He started working with songwriter Mario Martinelli and producer Roberto Morales. Later in 1994, Enrique contacted Fernan Martinez, who had once been Julio Iglesias's publicist. Enrique asked Martinez to help him get a record deal. "I thought the whole thing was suspicious, because he was Julio's son," Martinez recalled in *Teen People*. "But when I heard him [sing] I said, 'This is great. Let's get to work.' " However, there was one thing Enrique refused to do — use his famous last name to get a record contract. Instead, Enrique used the name Enrique Martinez when he sent off his demo tapes to record companies.

HIS FATHER'S SHADOW

Enrique has always loved his father, Julio. Still, when Enrique began making plans for his own music, he did not approach his father for either help or advice. Enrique's manager told MTV that "[Enrique] didn't want to be played on the radio [just] because he was Julio Iglesias's son." Enrique did not want to be known as "Julio's son" because people might not give him credit for his own talent. Enrique wanted to earn his success. And it was just a matter of time before that would happen.

Enrique loves and respects his father, Julio, but decided to start his career using the name Enrique Martinez.

CHAPTER TWO

Straight to the Top

"Please do not introduce me as the son of Julio Iglesias. I'm very proud of my father, but when you read Billboard now, you see Enrique Iglesias."

—Enrique in *People*

Enrique's demo tape was sent to several major U.S. record labels. One by one, the companies all turned down "Enrique Martinez." Finally, a small record label, Fonovisa, showed some interest. The label, which represents Mexican music, signed Enrique to a contract for three Spanish-language albums. Enrique was thrilled.

COMING TO TERMS

Enrique spent five months recording his first record in Toronto, Canada. He wrote and sang

Enrique began his singing career by recording only Spanish-language albums.

all of the songs in his native Spanish. When it came time to release the album, Enrique decided to drop the last name "Martinez" and use his true name: Iglesias. "[The name] is part of my blood, and heritage, and who I am," Enrique explained in the *Calgary Sun*. For this reason, Enrique decided to title the record *Enrique Iglesias*. He also dedicated the album to Elvira Olivares, thanking her for all of her help.

With the record complete, it was finally time for Enrique to tell his parents about his song-writing career. Unfortunately, before Enrique was able to tell his father, Julio found out the news at a music industry party. Enrique described his father's reaction to *Entertainment Weekly*. "He told me I was crazy," Enrique said. "As far as he knew, I wanted to be in business school." Enrique told Julio that he would not be returning to college, and that he was determined to become a singer. "I told [my father] I was sorry," Enrique recalled in *People*. "I said, 'Look, this is exactly what I've always wanted to do.' " When Julio finally calmed down and offered to help his son's career, Enrique stood firm. "Just let me do it my way, please," Enrique said.

SMASH SUCCESS

Enrique's decision to succeed on his own turned out to be a fortunate one. Released in October 1995, *Enrique Iglesias* was an instant hit, selling one million copies in the first three months of its release. Two singles on the album, "Si Tu Te Vas" and "Experiencia Religiosa," made the Top Ten on the Billboard Latin charts. Ironically, Julio's single, "Baila Morena," fell off the Billboard chart just as Enrique's first single, "Si Tu Te Vas," hit number one. Radio stations had fun playing up the rivalry between father and son. Enrique, however, insists that he and Julio have never been in competition with each other. Enrique

Enrique accepts a Grammy Award for
Best Latin Pop Performance.

told *Entertainment Weekly*, "He's my father. I respect him more than anything in the world. I love him more than anything in the world."

To date, *Enrique Iglesias* has sold six million copies. Even more impressive, Enrique was nominated for, and then won, the 1996 Grammy Award for Best Latin Pop Performance. Enrique became the best-selling Latin singer of 1996. All this, and he was just twenty-one years old!

MORE TO COME

With a hit debut album and a Grammy Award, it was hard to imagine how Enrique could do better the second time he made an album. He was ready for the challenge, though. In 1996, Enrique went back into the studio to

Did you know?

Enrique recorded his entire first album, *Enrique Iglesias*, in Italian as well as in Spanish. Enrique also has recorded music in Portuguese.

record his second Spanish-language album for the Fonovisa label. He decided to name his new record *Vivir*—the word "vivir" is Spanish for "to live."

Released in January 1997, *Vivir* was as big a success as was Enrique's first record. Just four months after its release, *Vivir* had gone platinum, selling one million copies. The record went on to sell more than five million copies.

It wasn't just romantic songwriting that was making Enrique a pop star. Women couldn't help but notice his stunning good looks. Fans were eager to see the sexy young star in person, crooning "Solo En Ti" ("Only in You") to his adoring audience. So in 1997, Enrique embarked on a world tour, which included seventy-eight concerts in thirteen countries. More than 700,000 fans turned out to see Enrique, making him one of the most popular Latin performers of all time.

During 1997, Enrique also appeared on many American television shows. He wanted to

Enrique won an American Music Award for Favorite Latin Artist in 1998.

bring his music to all people, not just the Spanish-speaking audience. Enrique appeared on "Late Night With David Letterman" and other talk shows. He also was featured on Kathie Lee Gifford's holiday special, "We Need A Little Christmas."

That same year, Enrique received nominations for Best Latin Performer at the Grammy Awards and the American Music Awards. He didn't win, but he was honored with *Billboard* magazine's Album of the Year. Enrique also picked up a Best Composer Award from ASCAP (American Society of Composers, Authors, and Publishers).

RUNAWAY SUCCESS

By early 1998, it was clear that there was no stopping Enrique's rise to music stardom. More people were becoming fans of his music. His concerts were selling out stadiums. The demand for new songs was greater than ever. While Enrique was hard at work on his third album, the Fonovisa label released an album of remixes to keep the fans happy. It featured old material mixed with new vocals and music so that the songs sounded different.

In September 1998, Enrique released his third album of new material in three years, *Cosas Del Amor* (The Things of Love). Although it was not as successful as were his first two records, Enrique's fans still loved what they heard. The album went gold, selling 500,000 copies in just six months. Enrique also picked up an American Music Award for Favorite Latin Artist that year.

At a record store, Enrique signs copies of his *Bailamos* CD.

NUMBER ONE

In 1999, superstar Will Smith was preparing the soundtrack for his film *Wild Wild West*. Smith took notice of the passion fans felt for Enrique. After attending one of Enrique's concerts, Smith recalled to MTV: "You've just never heard this kind of . . . screaming. I was like, I want this guy on the soundtrack."

Smith got his wish. Enrique recorded the song "Bailamos" (Spanish for "we dance") for the *Wild Wild West* soundtrack." The soundtrack quickly landed on the Billboard Top Ten chart. "Bailamos" also became the title track of Enrique's newest album, *Bailamos*. Released in June 1999, "Bailamos" went to number one on the Billboard Top Ten chart. *Bailamos* went gold three months later. In October 1999, another single off the album, "Esperanza," won a Latino Music Award for Song of the Year. Later that year, Fonovisa released *The Best Hits*, a greatest hits album that featured some of Enrique's best-loved songs, including "No Llores Por Mi" and "Bailamos."

MAKING IT IN ENGLISH

The album *Bailamos* marked the end of Enrique's contract with the Fonovisa label. Several U.S. record labels had begun making offers to Enrique. He decided to sign with Universal Music Group, which signed him to a six-album deal. Enrique would finally be able to fulfill his dream of recording songs in English.

Enrique's first English-language hit was "Rhythm Divine."

To record the album, Enrique worked with music producers in studios all over the world. Patrick Leonard, who has produced music for Madonna, produced part of the album. Enrique also worked with David Foster. Foster has produced songs for superstars such as Mariah Carey and Celine Dion. For Enrique's album, Foster produced the duet "Could I Have This Kiss Forever," which featured Enrique and Whitney Houston. Enrique enjoyed the experience of working with Houston. "It was great," Enrique explained in an AOL online chat. "I grew up [listening to] her voice, and I am a big fan. She is amazing."

In November 1999, Enrique's first English-language album was released, titled *Enrique*. The first single from the album was "Rhythm Divine." *Enrique* featured the song "Bailamos." The record also included a cover of a song by one of Enrique's songwriting idols, Bruce Springsteen.

"Rhythm Divine" hit the Top Ten on the American pop music charts in January 2000. In February, Enrique was nominated for four Billboard Latin Music Awards. In May, a third Enrique single, "Be With You," hit the American Top Ten. One month later, his duet with Whitney Houston, "Could I Have This Kiss Forever," was in the Top Forty.

CROSSING OVER

Enrique is one of a number of Latin performers who recently has had success in the English-language market. Music critics often call these performers "crossovers," meaning that the music appeals to both English- and Spanish-language audiences. Other crossover artists include Ricky Martin, Jennifer Lopez, and Marc Anthony. However, many artists don't like to be categorized as crossovers. They feel that the label separates their music from the mainstream. Speaking about *Enrique*,

Enrique told AOL: "I don't feel that it is a crossover album. I write and sing in both English and Spanish."

Though he is often compared to Ricky Martin, Enrique feels there is room for both artists to be successful. "There can't be just one Latin singer out there," Enrique told *Entertainment Weekly*. In *Teen People,* he also pointed out: "Musically, Ricky and I are completely different. He's Caribbean; I'm Mediterranean."

Beautiful Music

Enrique has written or cowritten many of the songs on his albums. The process of songwriting has always been a very personal one. It has not changed much since he was a shy young boy writing alone in his room late at night. Enrique even keeps the same schedule—writing through the night until 7:00 A.M. and sleeping until noon.

Enrique has many songwriting influences. His idols growing up were Bruce Springsteen, Billy Joel, Dire Straits, and Lionel Richie. He also admired the ballads of rock groups such as Foreigner and Journey.

Enrique also has been influenced by Latin music. "There's so many different [Latin] styles," Enrique told MTV. "There's flamenco, there's salsa, there's mambo, there's merengue, there's mainstream pop." Many of these styles make appearances on Enrique's albums, but his music is not easily categorized. Enrique likes it that way: "I have the best of both worlds. I can do English and I can do Spanish."

Enrique loves performing for his fans.

CHAPTER THREE

Fame, Family, and the Real Enrique

"I'm in a privileged position right now, and just being able to do what I love is amazing."
—Enrique in *YM*

Standing 6' 2" tall, Enrique is a handsome man who turns heads wherever he goes. In 1998, he was named "The Sexiest Man Alive" by *People en Español*. He also was featured in *People* magazine's "50 Most Beautiful People" issue that same year.

Enrique handles fame well. He tries to lead as normal a life as possible. Many of his closest friends are people he has known since elementary school or junior high. Some of those friends work with him on various projects.

Enrique was one of the performers during MTV's Fashionably Loud Contest.

Enrique lives in Miami, in a four-bedroom Mediterranean-style house that looks out on Biscayne Bay. Enrique had the house built in the same neighborhood that he lived in when he was a teenager. His friend and former nanny, Elvira Olivares, runs his household.

Enrique's siblings have had fulfilling lives, too. His older brother, Julio Jr., is now a singer. Julio Jr.'s first album, *Under My Eyes*, came out in 2000. Julio Jr. also recorded a song for the soundtrack for the film *Music of the Heart*, starring Meryl Streep and Gloria Estefan. Julio Jr. was the opening act for part of Cher's "Believe" tour in 1999. Enrique's sister, Chabeli, is the host of a Spanish-language television show.

BEACH BOY

When he is not recording or touring the world, Enrique enjoys hanging out with his friends. He loves Miami and loves all kinds of water

Enrique and Boy George are close friends.

sports. Fishing, scuba diving, and waterskiing are big favorites. He is even a bit of a daredevil. One time, Enrique was careless while waterskiing and smacked into a mango tree. He had to have forty stitches to reattach his left ear! Enrique also has started hang gliding and is taking flying lessons.

LOOKING FOR LOVE

Enrique is a true romantic. Many of the ballads he has written are about lost love, or love gone wrong. He is still looking for the true love of his life: "I want a girl who's a little bit on the wild side," Enrique told *InStyle*.

When Enrique finds love, he is sure that it will be with one special person. "I just want to have one girlfriend," he told *People*. Enrique is attracted to women who are independent and who have their own talents. He also knows that part of the price of his fame is that it's hard for him to trust people. That makes finding the

Enrique is just friends with Shannon Elizabeth, the star of his video "Be With You."

right girl difficult. Enrique is well aware that some women might be attracted to him because of his fame and money rather than for himself. "That's one thing I know. You can tell if they like you for yourself," he told *Teen People*.

Enrique admits that his busy schedule makes dating difficult. In an interview with

Enrique is devoted to his fans.

MTV's Carson Daly, Enrique said that the hardest thing about dating is "dealing with my schedule and finding a free day to do something." He hasn't given up, though. Enrique hopes to find the right girl and get married someday.

Another drawback to Enrique's fame is the lack of privacy. Anytime Enrique goes out in public, he is likely to be crowded by fans. "You become a little freaky about going out in public," he explained to *Teen People*. "If I'm walking down the street and people start screaming, I get really embarrassed."

Y2K

Enrique's career just keeps getting bigger. He performed as part of the show at Super Bowl XXXIV in January 2000. In April of that year, Enrique appeared on VH1's "Men Strike Back" concert, performing a duet with the famous singer Tom Jones. That same month, he won a

Billboard Latin Music Award for Hot Latin Tracks Artist of the Year. In May, Enrique picked up the award for Favorite Latino Artist at the Blockbuster Awards. He performed on the "Rosie O' Donnell Show" and with opera star Luciano Pavarotti on the TV special "Pavarotti & Friends."

In June 2000, radio talk-show host Howard Stern accused Enrique of lip-synching on a television show. Enrique denied the rumor and appeared on Stern's show to sing "Rhythm Divine" live. Of course, he sang beautifully, and the rumor was quickly put to rest.

Enrique tours regularly and remains devoted to his millions of fans. He encourages them to pursue their own dreams. In an AOL chat, Enrique advised, "I know it sounds corny, but when you follow your dreams, it happens, and if it's music, take it seriously." Enrique wouldn't do it any other way.

Enrique performed at VH1's "Men Strike Back" concert.

TIMELINE

1975   •Enrique Iglesias is born in Madrid, Spain.

1984   •Enrique and his siblings leave Spain to live in Miami, Florida, with their father.

1988   •Enrique writes his first song at the age of thirteen.

1993   •Enrique graduates from high school.
         •Enrique records his demo tape.

1995   •The album *Enrique Iglesias* is released on the Fonovisa record label.

1996   •Enrique wins a Grammy Award for Best Latin Pop Performance.

1997   •*Vivir*, Enrique's second album, is released.
         •Within months of the release of *Vivir*, the record goes platinum.

TIMELINE

1998
- *Cosas Del Amor* is released.
- Enrique wins an American Music Award for Favorite Latin Artist.
- *People en Espanol* names Enrique The Sexiest Man Alive.
- Enrique is featured in *People* magazine's "50 Most Beautiful People" issue.

1999
- The *Wild Wild West* soundtrack is released.
- *Bailamos* is released in June.
- In October, the song "Esperanza" wins a Ritmo Latino Music Award for song of the year.
- In November, Enrique's first English-language album, *Enrique*, is released.

2000
- In January, Enrique performs at the Super Bowl XXXIV.
- The song "Rhythm Divine" hits the American Top Ten.

TIMELINE

2000
- In April, Enrique appears on the VH1 special "Men Strike Back."
- In April, Enrique wins a Billboard Latin Music Award for Hot Latin Tracks Artist of the Year.
- Enrique is nominated for an American Music Award for Favorite Latin Artist.
- In May, Enrique picks up the award for Favorite Latino Artist at the Blockbuster Awards.
- Enrique performs on the "Rosie O' Donnell Show."
- Enrique sings with opera star Luciano Pavarotti on the TV special "Pavarotti & Friends."
- Enrique performs on the Howard Stern radio talk show.

FACT SHEET

Name	Enrique Iglesias
Born	May 8, 1975
Birthplace	Madrid, Spain
Family	Julio Iglesias, father; Isabel Preysler, mother; Julio Jr., brother; Chabeli, sister
Height	6' 2"
Pet	Grammy, a golden retriever
Car	Silver 1998 SUV

Favorites

Actors	Anthony Hopkins, Keanu Reeves
Book	*The Old Man and the Sea*
Colors	Black, white, red, gray
Foods	Chicken McNuggets, hamburgers, pizza, sushi
Movie	*Raiders of the Lost Ark*
Sports	hang gliding, scuba diving, waterskiing, windsurfing
Musicians	Dire Straits, Lionel Richie, Bruce Springsteen
Author	Ernest Hemingway

NEW WORDS

chart a listing that ranks music sales

demo tape a music recording made to present a song to a record label

duet a song for two performers

flamenco a dance style of the Spanish Gypsies

gold record a certificate awarded to an album or a single that sells 500,000 copies

Grammy Award an award given in recognition of musical achievement

mambo a ballroom dance of Cuban origin that is similar to the cha-cha

merengue a ballroom dance of Haitian and Dominican origin

nomination the selection of someone for an award

NEW WORDS

platinum record a certificate awarded to an album or a single that sells one million copies

pop relating to popular music

producer the person who supervises the production of a record, film, or television program

record label a company that produces and sells records

salsa popular music of Latin American origin that has absorbed characteristics of rhythm and blues, jazz, and rock

soundtrack the music recorded for a movie

FOR FURTHER READING

Anne-Johns, Michael and Catherine Murphy. *Enrique Iglesias*. Kansas City, MO: Andrews & McMeel Publishing, 2000.

Furman, Elina and Leah Furman. *Enrique Iglesias*. New York: St. Martin's Press, 2000.

Krulik, Nancy E. *Pop Goes Latin!* New York: The Putnam Publishing Group, 1999.

Lockyer, Daphne. *Julio: The Unsung Story*. Secaucus, NJ: Carol Publishing Group, 1997.

RESOURCES

Enrique
www.enriqueig.com
This is the Interscope Records' official Enrique Web site. It contains a bio, sound clips, and messages from Enrique. It also includes current news about Enrique's appearances and performances.

Rock On The Net: Enrique Iglesias
www.rockonthenet.com/artists-i/ enriqueiglesias_main.htm
This site contains information about Enrique, including a timeline, a discography, and a bio. There are links to learn more about Enrique.

SonicNet Music Guide
www.sonicnet.com/guide/search_frame.jhtml ?query=enrique+iglesias
SonicNet provides information about many different artists, including Enrique. The site contains recent new articles, audio clips, and album reviews. Check out the Enrique bulletin board to hear what other fans have to say.

INDEX

About the Author

Morgan Talmadge is a freelance writer and soccer coach living in Mt. Vernon, Iowa.